Following PROTOCOL ... or NOT?!

A straight-forward and concise primer on contemporary antisemitism today

drafted by

A Group of Concerned Upstanders

Published by ISGAP
www.isgap.org
info@isgap.org

ISBN 979-8-323888-40-5 *(Paperback)*
ISBN 978-1-940186-20-7 *(Kindle)*

Following Protocol ... or Not?! A Straight-Forward and Concise Primer on Contemporary Antisemitism Today

First edition 2024
© This edition is copyrighted in all countries.

All rights reserved. No part of this publication may be reproduced, translated, stored in a retrieval system, or transmitted in any form or by any means, electronic, mechanical, photocopying, recording or otherwise, without prior permission from the author and publisher.

The Institute for the Study of Global Antisemitism and Policy (ISGAP) is dedicated to the academic study of antisemitism and others forms of prejudice. The opinions expressed in this work are those of the author and do not necessarily reflect the views of ISGAP, its officers, or the members of its boards.

Cover image: Naomi Blake (1924-2007, British sculptor and Holocaust survivor), *Phoenix II*, 1986, bronze maquette, private collection.

"Antisemitism is not a parochial Jewish, Israeli, or Zionist problem. It's a problem for humanity."

— Charles Asher Small
Founder and Executive Director of the Institute for the Study of Global Antisemitism and Policy

"Unlike most other prejudices, which tend to come from one place in the political spectrum, certainly ethnic, religious prejudices, antisemitism cuts across all boundaries."

— Deborah Lipstadt
US Special Envoy to Monitor and Combat Antisemitism

PREFACE

A Group of Concerned Upstanders

In the pursuit of advancing critical contemporary antisemitism studies as a recognized academic discipline, the Institute for the Study of Global Antisemitism and Policy (ISGAP) is unwavering in its dedication. This commitment finds expression in the creation of the learning resource presented in this primer, entitled *Following Protocol... or Not?!*

The genesis of *Following Protocol* can be traced back to the influential work initiated at the ISGAP-Oxford Summer Institute for Curriculum Development in Critical Contemporary Antisemitism Studies. This weeklong intensive program, conducted under the guidance of globally recognized scholars, took place under the auspices of ISGAP.

The narrative of *Following Protocol* unfolds from profound discussions ignited by two friends endeavoring to reconcile thought and action within their respective—and our shared—worlds. The overarching goal was to deepen our understanding of and actively combat the growing scourge of contemporary antisemitism.

The project gained substantial form and substance through the invaluable contributions of numerous scholars associated with ISGAP. Their expertise, experience, and passionate commitment have played a pivotal role in shaping and developing this endeavor, making a positive impact in the present moment. Furthermore, we acknowledge the insights garnered from AI bots such as ChatGPT and Perplexity, underscoring the collaborative and interdisciplinary nature of this project.

As the ISGAP Team presents this work to you, our readers, we express our utmost gratitude for the timely realization of this project. May *Following Protocol... or Not?!* serve as a meaningful contribution to the ongoing discourse surrounding contemporary antisemitism studies.

INTRODUCTION

(2024)

This primer is the result of deep and broad discussions among a diverse team of international scholars and educators with a passionate focus on the who, what, when, why, and how of contemporary antisemitism. After months of diving into topics and reorganizing ideas, it became clear that a straight-forward explanation of what "typical" people need to know about contemporary antisemitism today was needed by all, desperately. Its simplistic form is modeled on the cheap, widely distributed 1933 pamphlet that catapulted Jew hatred into the mainstream and continues to catalyze the ever-changing mutations and complexities of modern antisemitism: the fictitious *Protocols of the Elders of Zion*.

Understanding contemporary antisemitism is important for fostering tolerance, combating discrimination, and promoting a just and inclusive society. In summary, everyone generally should know about the following key elements about contemporary antisemitism:

- **Definition of Antisemitism:** Antisemitism is hatred, prejudice, or discrimination against Jews based on their religion or ethnicity. It can manifest in various forms, from verbal abuse and stereotypes to physical violence and institutional bias.
- **Historical Context:** Recognize the historical roots of antisemitism, including the long history of persecution, pogroms, and the Holocaust. Understanding this history provides crucial context for contemporary manifestations.
- **Contemporary Forms:** Antisemitism has evolved. It can now take the form of conspiracy theories (e.g., Jewish control of the media or world governments), Holocaust denial, and anti-Israel sentiments that cross into anti-Jewish sentiment.

- **Online Hate:** The Internet has amplified the spread of antisemitism. Social media platforms, in particular, can be breeding grounds for hateful content and harassment against Jews.
- **Intersectionality:** Antisemitism can intersect with other forms of prejudice, such as racism, xenophobia, and discrimination based on sexual orientation or gender identity. Understanding this helps in combating multiple forms of hatred.
- **Criticism vs. Antisemitism:** It's essential to distinguish between legitimate criticism of the Israeli government's policies and antisemitism. Criticism becomes antisemitic when it employs stereotypes, conspiracies, or generalized blame against all Jews.
- **Educational Efforts:** Many organizations and institutions work to educate people about antisemitism. Be open to learning about it from reliable sources.
- **Reporting Hate:** Encourage people to report incidents of antisemitism to the appropriate authorities or organizations. Reporting helps track and combat hate crimes.
- **Support for Victims:** Show empathy and support for victims of antisemitism. As with any form of discrimination, solidarity is crucial.
- **Promote Tolerance and Inclusivity:** Actively promote a society that values diversity and inclusivity. Combating antisemitism is part of a broader effort to create a world where everyone is treated with dignity and respect.
- **Laws against Hate:** Be aware of laws in your country that address hate speech and hate crimes. Advocate for the enforcement and strengthening of these laws where necessary.
- **Engage in Dialogue:** Engage in open and respectful dialogue with people from different backgrounds and perspectives. This can help break down stereotypes and build bridges of understanding.
- **Support Organizations:** Support organizations and initiatives that work to combat antisemitism and promote tolerance, both locally and internationally.

Practically, the primer starts with a working definition of contemporary antisemitism (section 1), followed by 20 statements in four areas. Statements I-V introduce the "big lie." In the context of Nazi propaganda and antisemitism, this refers to the false and malicious belief that Jews were responsible for many of society's problems, particularly economic and political troubles. This lie was used as a foundational element in promoting anti-Jewish sentiment, discrimination, and, ultimately, the Holocaust. The phrase was popularized in Adolf Hitler's book *Mein Kampf*, in which he accused Jews of using a "lie so colossal" that people would not believe that others "could have the impudence to distort the truth so infamously." The term "big lie" is often invoked in discussions about antisemitism to highlight how dangerous and destructive false stereotypes and conspiracy theories can be when they are used to scapegoat and vilify an entire group of people. It serves as a reminder of the tragic consequences that can arise when such hateful ideas are allowed to spread unchecked.

Statements VI-X specifically address the fictitious *Protocols of the Elders of Zion*. It is a fabricated text that first emerged in the early 20th century, in Russia. It purports to be a secret plan by Jewish leaders to control the world, manipulate governments, and exploit non-Jews. This document is widely regarded as a hoax and has been debunked numerous times. It was originally created as antisemitic propaganda and was used to justify persecution and discrimination against Jewish communities. In contemporary times, the *Protocols* continues to be utilized by antisemitic individuals and groups to promote their agenda.

Statements XI-XV discuss common misconceptions about antisemitism that perpetuate hatred, prejudice, and discrimination against Jewish people. Statements XVI-XX suggest ways to "break" the inherent, subconscious, and deliberate "protocols" of contemporary antisemitism with vigilance in countering these false narratives and promoting tolerance, diversity, and understanding. Finally, recommended techniques, strategies, and resources for combating contemporary antisemitism are provided for further exploration (sections 2, 3, and 4).

This brief, high-level overview is intended to serve as a starting point. Antisemitism is an enormous issue with a long history. In overt and covert ways, current manifestations of and trends in contemporary antisemitism threaten most every aspect of our global society—*everywhere, every day*. Educating oneself and others about contemporary antisemitism is a crucial step toward building a more inclusive and just society. It's not just about protecting one group; it's about safeguarding the principles of equality and respect for all.

1. CONTEMPORARY ANTISEMITISM

The term "antisemitism" has evolved over time in its meaning and connotations, reflecting changes in society, politics, and our understanding of discrimination and prejudice. It is important to note that "antisemitism" specifically refers to prejudice against Jews, even though the term itself can be somewhat misleading since it suggests hostility toward all Semitic peoples when hyphenated (anti-Semitism, anti-Semite).

Historical Roots

The historical roots of antisemitism are complex and multifaceted, spanning thousands of years. As an ideology, antisemitism has evolved and taken different forms throughout history, adapting to the cultural, political, and social contexts of different societies. Its roots are deeply embedded in history, making it a complex and enduring problem that continues to be a concern today. Efforts to combat antisemitism require understanding its historical foundations and addressing its contemporary manifestations. While it's challenging to pinpoint a single foundation for antisemitism, there are several key historical events and factors that have contributed to its development over time. Here is a brief overview of some of the foundational elements.

- **Religious Factors:** Much of the early antisemitism can be traced back to religious differences and tensions. The Jewish people's refusal to adopt the dominant religious beliefs of the societies they lived in often led to suspicions and hostilities. For example, in ancient Egypt, the Hebrews' refusal to worship Egyptian gods led to their enslavement.
- **Ancient Stereotypes:** Stereotypes about Jews began to emerge in ancient times. These stereotypes often portrayed Jews as outsiders, moneylenders, or conspirators, contributing to negative perceptions. The portrayal of Jews as "Christ-killers" in Christian theology played a significant role in medieval antisemitism.
- **Economic Factors:** Jews have been involved in various economic activities throughout history, including money lending and trade. In many cases, they were forced into these roles due to restrictions on land ownership and other professions. This economic involvement led

to resentment and jealousy, with Jews being scapegoated for economic troubles.
- **Medieval Europe:** Antisemitism became deeply ingrained in European society during the Middle Ages. Jews were often subjected to persecution, expulsion, and violence, for example during the Crusades and the Spanish Inquisition.
- **Blood Libel and Ritual Accusations:** False accusations of Jews using the blood of Christian children in religious rituals (blood libel) became prevalent in medieval Europe and continued in various forms for centuries. These baseless accusations fueled hatred and violence against Jewish communities.
- **The Black Death:** During the Black Death in the 14th century, Jews were falsely blamed for spreading the plague, leading to widespread persecution and massacres.
- **Enlightenment and Modern Antisemitism:** Even as societies in Europe became more secular and enlightened, antisemitism persisted. Enlightenment thinkers like Voltaire and Kant held prejudiced views against Jews. In the 19th and 20th centuries, pseudoscientific theories about racial superiority, such as those promoted by the Nazis, further fueled antisemitism and ultimately led to the Holocaust.
- **Political and Social Factors:** Antisemitism was exploited for political purposes in various periods, including the Russian pogroms and the rise of the Nazi regime in Germany. Jews were often blamed for social and political problems, serving as convenient scapegoats.
- **Zionism and the State of Israel:** The establishment of the State of Israel in 1948 has also had an impact on antisemitism. Some individuals and groups use criticism of Israel as a cover for antisemitic beliefs and actions.

Evolutionary Timeline

Part of the complexity of antisemitism today lies in the fact that the meaning of "antisemitism" has evolved from its origins as a term denoting religious, racial, and ethnic hatred of Jews to encompass a broader range of prejudices and discriminatory behaviors. It reflects society's changing understanding of discrimination and its commitment to combating all forms of hatred and bigotry. However, debates about where legitimate criticism of Israeli policies ends and antisemitism begins continue to shape discussions around this term.

1. **Origins (19th Century):** The term "antisemitism" was coined in the 19th century, in Germany, by Wilhelm Marr. At this time, it referred to a specific form of racial and ethnic hatred directed against Jews. It was rooted in pseudo-scientific notions of racial purity and superiority, and it often framed Jews as a threat to the Aryan race.
2. **Late 19th to Early 20th Century:** Antisemitism evolved during this period into a widespread social and political movement, particularly in Europe. It was characterized by discriminatory laws, pogroms, and stereotypes about Jewish people being responsible for various societal problems. Notably, the Dreyfus Affair in France and the *Protocols of the Elders of Zion*, a fabricated antisemitic text, contributed to the spread of this prejudice.
3. **Holocaust and Post-World War II:** The Holocaust, in which over six million Jews were systematically murdered by the Nazis, revealed the devastating consequences of antisemitism. After World War II, there was a growing awareness of the need to combat antisemitism and promote tolerance. In 1948, the United Nations first adopted the Convention on the Prevention and Punishment of the Crime of Genocide, followed by the Universal Declaration of Human Rights, which explicitly condemned discrimination on the basis of religion.
4. **Late 20th Century:** The meaning of antisemitism broadened in the late 20th century to include not just explicit acts of violence or discrimination against Jews but also more subtle forms of prejudice, such as stereotypes, biased language, and microaggressions. This broader definition recognized that antisemitism could manifest in cultural, social, and economic spheres, as well as through political means.
5. **Contemporary Understanding:** In contemporary discussions, antisemitism encompasses various manifestations, including classic religious and ethnic prejudices against Jews, Holocaust denial or distortion, conspiracy theories about Jewish control or influence, and criticism of Israel that crosses into antisemitic tropes and anti-Zionist demands for the dismantling of the State of Israel. The line between legitimate criticism of Israeli policies and antisemitism is a subject of debate.
6. **Intersectionality:** Antisemitism is sometimes examined in the context of intersectionality, recognizing that individuals may experience multiple forms of discrimination simultaneously. For example, some Jews face discrimination not only based on their religion but also due to their ethnicity or other aspects of their identity.

7. ***Efforts to Combat Antisemitism:*** International organizations, governments, and advocacy groups have made efforts to combat antisemitism through education, legislation, and awareness campaigns. The International Holocaust Remembrance Alliance (IHRA) has formulated a working definition of antisemitism that has been adopted by several countries and organizations.

IHRA Working Definition

The IHRA (International Holocaust Remembrance Alliance) working definition of antisemitism is significant because it provides a widely accepted and comprehensive framework for identifying and addressing antisemitism. It helps governments, organizations, and individuals recognize and combat various forms of antisemitism, fostering a common understanding that can contribute to the prevention of discrimination and hate crimes against Jewish people. Additionally, it promotes international cooperation and solidarity in the fight against antisemitism. Adopted on May 26, 2016, the full text of the working definition of antisemitism (reproduced below) appears on the IHRA website.

"Antisemitism is a certain perception of Jews, which may be expressed as hatred toward Jews. Rhetorical and physical manifestations of antisemitism are directed toward Jewish or non-Jewish individuals and/or their property, toward Jewish community institutions and religious facilities."

To guide IHRA in its work, the following examples may serve as illustrations:

Manifestations might include the targeting of the state of Israel, conceived as a Jewish collectivity. However, criticism of Israel similar to that leveled against any other country cannot be regarded as antisemitic. Antisemitism frequently charges Jews with conspiring to harm humanity, and it is often used to blame Jews for "why things go wrong." It is expressed in speech, writing, visual forms and action, and employs sinister stereotypes and negative character traits.

Contemporary examples of antisemitism in public life, the media, schools, the workplace, and in the religious sphere could, taking into account the overall context, include, but are not limited to:

- Calling for, aiding, or justifying the killing or harming of Jews in the name of a radical ideology or an extremist view of religion.

- Making mendacious, dehumanizing, demonizing, or stereotypical allegations about Jews as such or the power of Jews as collective — such as, especially but not exclusively, the myth about a world Jewish conspiracy or of Jews controlling the media, economy, government or other societal institutions.

- Accusing Jews as a people of being responsible for real or imagined wrongdoing committed by a single Jewish person or group, or even for acts committed by non-Jews.

- Denying the fact, scope, mechanisms (e.g. gas chambers) or intentionality of the genocide of the Jewish people at the hands of National Socialist Germany and its supporters and accomplices during World War II (the Holocaust).

- Accusing the Jews as a people, or Israel as a state, of inventing or exaggerating the Holocaust.

- Accusing Jewish citizens of being more loyal to Israel, or to the alleged priorities of Jews worldwide, than to the interests of their own nations.

- Denying the Jewish people their right to self-determination, e.g., by claiming that the existence of a State of Israel is a racist endeavor.

- Applying double standards by requiring of it a behavior not expected or demanded of any other democratic nation.

- Using the symbols and images associated with classic antisemitism (e.g., claims of Jews killing Jesus or blood libel) to characterize Israel or Israelis.

- Drawing comparisons of contemporary Israeli policy to that of the Nazis.

- Holding Jews collectively responsible for actions of the state of Israel.

Antisemitic acts are criminal when they are so defined by law (for example, denial of the Holocaust or distribution of antisemitic materials in some countries).

Criminal acts are antisemitic when the targets of attacks, whether they are people or property—such as buildings, schools, places of worship and cemeteries—are selected because they are, or are perceived to be, Jewish or linked to Jews.

Antisemitic discrimination is the denial to Jews of opportunities or services available to others and is illegal in many countries.

Following
PROTOCOL
... or NOT?!

I
Antisemitism is the only form of racism that's grounded in a conspiracy theory.

This matters because antisemitism's being rooted in conspiracy theories can lead to widespread misinformation, prejudice, and harmful stereotypes against Jewish people. (The *Protocols of the Elders of Zion* is a notorious antisemitic hoax that claims to describe a global conspiracy by Jewish leaders to control the world.) These conspiracy theories have historically fueled discrimination, hatred, and even violence. Understanding this unique aspect of antisemitism helps address its origins and work toward combating its negative impact on society.

II
Antisemitism started with the Jews, but it won't end with the Jews...

Elie Wiesel's statement, "Antisemitism started with the Jews, but it will not end with the Jews," reflects a deeper understanding of the historical roots and nature of antisemitism. This quote suggests that, while the prejudice and hostility against Jewish people might have originated from misconceptions, stereotypes, and historical conflicts involving Jews, antisemitism has grown beyond its origins to become a broader and more pervasive form of discrimination that affects not only Jews but also society as a whole.

By stating that antisemitism won't end with the Jews, Wiesel is highlighting the fact that prejudice and discrimination against a particular group can have ripple effects, influencing other forms of bigotry and intolerance. The sentiment behind the statement is that the hatred and intolerance directed at Jews are indicative of a larger issue within society—the capacity for people to target and discriminate against any group based on differences, be they religious, ethnic, racial, or cultural.

In essence, Wiesel is underscoring the idea that combating antisemitism requires addressing the underlying issues of prejudice and discrimination that affect all marginalized and targeted groups. The statement serves as a reminder that confronting antisemitism isn't just about protecting Jewish people; it's about addressing a more profound societal problem of hatred and intolerance that has the potential to harm many groups.

Ultimately, the quote reflects Wiesel's belief in the interconnectedness of all forms of discrimination and the necessity of working toward a more inclusive and tolerant society that rejects prejudice in all its manifestations.

III
While propaganda isn't always negative, the *Protocols of the Elders of Zion* is an example of the worst kind of propaganda.

"Black propaganda" refers to false information or narratives deliberately spread with the intention to deceive, mislead, and manipulate. It often involves the creation of fabricated stories, documents, or evidence to promote a particular agenda or discredit a certain group or individual. Two key characteristics of black propaganda include disguising the source or author of the work, in order to create the impression that it was created by those it is supposed to discredit, and presenting the content in a legitimate form to reinforce its "credibility" and to extend its influence.

The *Protocols of the Elders of Zion* is a notorious example of black propaganda. It is a fabricated text that claims to detail a global conspiracy by supposed Jewish leaders to control the world. This document was first published in the early 20th century and has been widely debunked as a forgery and antisemitic piece of pure fiction. Despite its lack of credibility, it has been—*and continues to be*—used as a tool to promote hatred, discrimination, and violence against Jewish communities.

The negative implications of black propaganda include:

1. ***Spreading Falsehoods:*** Black propaganda intentionally spreads false information, which can lead to the dissemination of harmful and malicious narratives. This can result in social division, prejudice, and even violence against targeted groups.
2. ***Undermining Trust:*** The use of black propaganda erodes trust in information sources, making it harder for people to discern fact from

fiction. This can lead to a general sense of confusion and skepticism, which can harm democratic societies reliant on accurate information.
3. **Fueling Hate and Prejudice:** Black propaganda, especially when it targets a specific group or community, can exacerbate existing prejudices and hatred. In the case of the *Protocols*, it has fueled antisemitic sentiments and contributed to historical and contemporary discrimination against Jewish individuals and communities.
4. **Manipulating Public Opinion:** Black propaganda is designed to manipulate public opinion to serve the interests of those spreading it. This can lead to the adoption of policies or actions that are based on falsehoods, which may have serious consequences for individuals and societies.

Understanding the implications of black propaganda, as exemplified by the *Protocols*, highlights the dangers of intentionally spreading false information to manipulate public opinion and promote hatred. It underscores the importance of critical thinking, media literacy, and responsible information consumption to counter the negative effects of such propaganda.

IV
The core of contemporary antisemitism, the *Protocols* is a fabricated story that blames the Jewish people for all of the world's problems.

A notorious antisemitic forgery that was first published in Russia in the early 20th century, in 1903, the *Protocols of the Elders of Zion* purports to be a secret plan created by a group of Jewish elders to control the world by manipulating finance, media, and politics. It falsely claims that Jewish people are plotting to achieve global domination and exploit non-Jewish populations. Despite being debunked as a hoax multiple times (around the world and even in Russia), the text continues to circulate and has had a significant impact on the history of antisemitism.

Here's how the *Protocols* laid the foundation for contemporary antisemitism.

- **Promotion of Stereotypes:** The *Protocols* perpetuated harmful stereotypes about Jewish people, portraying them as cunning, manipulative, and power-hungry. This reinforced existing prejudices and contributed to the scapegoating of Jews for various societal problems.

- **Validation of Prejudices:** The text offered a seemingly authoritative and secret explanation for complex world events, validating existing prejudices and providing a convenient scapegoat for societal problems. This made it easier for individuals to blame Jewish people for issues beyond their control.
- **Global Conspiracy Theory:** The idea of a secret Jewish cabal working behind the scenes to control world affairs played into a broader narrative of global conspiracy theories. This resonated with individuals who were already prone to believing in such conspiracies.
- **Pseudo-Academic Appearance:** The *Protocols* was presented as a serious document, employing a pseudo-academic tone that gave it an air of legitimacy. This made it more challenging for people to immediately dismiss it as a hoax.
- **Spread through Propaganda:** The text was widely disseminated through propaganda efforts and translated into numerous languages, enabling it to reach a global audience. Its wide distribution helped it gain traction and contributed to its global influence.
- **Impact on Public Opinion:** The *Protocols* influenced public opinion and became a rallying point for various antisemitic movements. It fueled hatred, bigotry, and discrimination against Jewish communities.
- **Influence on Hate Groups:** The narrative of Jewish world domination outlined in the *Protocols* provided hate groups and extremist organizations with a rallying cry and a justification for their antisemitic activities.
- **Perpetuation of Antisemitic Beliefs:** Even after being exposed as a forgery, the *Protocols* continued to find believers who were willing to accept its claims. This perpetuated antisemitic beliefs and attitudes across generations.
- **Media and Pop Culture:** The ideas from the *Protocols* have been incorporated into various forms of media and pop culture, further cementing its influence on public opinion.

In this way, the *Protocols* played a significant role in laying the foundations for contemporary antisemitism by promoting harmful stereotypes, providing a seemingly authoritative explanation for complex issues, and serving as a rallying point for hate groups. Its enduring impact underscores the importance of countering false narratives and promoting understanding and tolerance among different communities.

V
As Henry Ford said, "they [the *Protocols*] fit in with what is going on," but if you *think* about it they're just a "convenient" excuse for other factors.

Henry Ford was an influential American industrialist and the founder of the Ford Motor Company. In the early 1920s, Ford's newspaper, *The Dearborn Independent*, published a series of articles that promoted antisemitic ideas and conspiracy theories, often relying on the *Protocols* as a source. In fact, *The Dearborn Independent* published a series called "The International Jew: The World's Problem," which compiled and endorsed antisemitic views, including those found in the *Protocols*.

Ford's involvement in promoting these ideas is complex, and his motivations can be debated. Some historians suggest that he might have genuinely believed in the authenticity of the *Protocols* due to his antisemitic biases, while others argue that he saw it as a tool to further his own political and economic goals. It's important to note that the *Protocols* had been widely discredited as a forgery by this time, even though they continued to circulate and be used to fuel antisemitic sentiments.

Henry Ford's actions and words during this period have been widely criticized for their contribution to the spread of antisemitic propaganda. He eventually issued an apology and distanced himself from *The Dearborn Independent*'s articles in the mid-1920s after losing a million-dollar libel case and a public backlash. However, the damage caused by his promotion of such harmful ideas had already been done.

VI
The *Protocols* was crafted to protect the Russian Tsar's political position.

The *Protocols of the Elders of Zion* was first published in Russia in the early 20th century and gained significant traction, especially in antisemitic and nationalist circles. While it's true that the text was used to advance various political agendas, including protecting the Russian Tsar's political position, it's important to note that the document itself is fabricated and has been widely discredited as a forgery.

The exact origins of the *Protocols* are not entirely clear, but it is widely believed to have been created by Russian secret police officials, particularly the Okhrana, in the late 19th century. The intent behind crafting the document was to shift blame and resentment for the political and economic issues facing Russia onto a scapegoat—Jews and a supposed global Jewish conspiracy. The publication of the *Protocols* aimed to achieve several objectives, including:

1. ***Diversion of Blame:*** Russia was facing internal turmoil, social unrest, and economic challenges during the late 19th and early 20th centuries. The Tsarist regime sought to deflect public dissatisfaction by focusing public anger on a fabricated external enemy, thus diverting attention away from the government's own failures.
2. ***Legitimization of Repression:*** By creating the narrative of a Jewish conspiracy to control the world, the authorities could justify increased surveillance, repression, and discrimination against Jews within Russia. The Tsar's government could use the document as a pretext for introducing or maintaining repressive policies and measures.
3. ***Consolidation of Support:*** The publication of the *Protocols* was intended to rally nationalist and antisemitic factions around the Tsar. By presenting a common enemy, the regime could potentially garner support from those who believed in the conspiracy, strengthening the position of the monarchy.

Scholars and experts have conclusively proven that the *Protocols* is a plagiarized and distorted version of earlier fictional works, including a French political satire called *Dialogue aux enfers entre Machiavel et Montesquieu* (Dialogue in Hell between Machiavelli and Montesquieu, 1864) and a fictional German story called "The Rabbi's Speech" (1868, later republished as a "factual" pamphlet). The text has no basis in reality and has been repeatedly exposed as a fraudulent piece of propaganda.

While the *Protocols of the Elders of Zion* was indeed used as a tool to support the Russian Tsar's political position by redirecting public grievances and justifying repression, the document itself is a malicious fabrication. It is a prime example of how propaganda and misinformation can be used to manipulate public opinion and serve political agendas.

VII
The simple pamphlet details a fictitious Jewish plot to take over the world.

The *Protocols of the Elders of Zion* is presented as a series of protocols or minutes from the secret meetings of a group of powerful Jews known as the "Elders of Zion." The pamphlet claims that these supposed Jewish leaders are plotting to achieve global dominance by manipulating political, economic, and social events. The *Protocols* outlines a series of strategies to undermine existing power structures, weaken nations, and establish a New World Order under Jewish control. These strategies include:

- ***Manipulating financial institutions:*** The *Protocols* suggests that Jews aim to gain control over banking and finance, thereby exerting influence over economies and governments.
- ***Discrediting traditional institutions:*** The *Protocols* proposes discrediting religious, political, and social institutions to create chaos and pave the way for the rise of the Jewish leadership.
- ***Exploiting cultural differences:*** The *Protocols* alleges that Jews plan to exploit existing tensions between different cultural and religious groups to further their agenda.
- ***Establishing puppet governments:*** The *Protocols* proposes the creation of puppet governments that could be easily manipulated by the alleged Jewish conspirators.
- ***Undermining social values:*** The *Protocols* suggests undermining traditional moral values and promoting behaviors that would lead to societal breakdown.

The *Protocols* pamphlet has been condemned by historians, scholars, courts, governments, and organizations around the world for its hateful and false content. It has played a significant role in fueling antisemitic conspiracy theories and has been used to justify discrimination, violence, and persecution against Jewish communities.

VIII
Numerous historical refutations prove that the 24 protocols are a hoax.

There are numerous historical and scholarly refutations that demonstrate the falseness of the *Protocols*. Here are some key points that highlight why the *Protocols* is considered a hoax.

1. *Source and Origins:* The origins of the *Protocols* can be traced back to the late 19th century. They first appeared in Russia as an appendix to *The Great in the Small* (1903) by Sergei Nilus. It is widely believed that the *Protocols* was fabricated by members of the Russian secret police (Okhrana) as a means to scapegoat and persecute Jews. This assertion is supported by historical evidence and investigations.
2. *Plagiarism and Borrowed Material:* Researchers have found that significant portions of the *Protocols* were lifted directly from various sources, including satirical literature, philosophical works, and political writings. Notably, sections were plagiarized from a French political satire called *Dialogue aux enfers entre Machiavel et Montesquieu* by Maurice Joly and a fictional German story called "The Rabbi's Speech" by Hermann Goedsche. This clear borrowing discredits the originality and authenticity of the *Protocols*.
3. *Anachronisms:* The *Protocols* contains references to events, technologies, and political ideologies that were not known or in existence at the time they were purportedly written (namely in the late 19th century). These anachronisms suggest that the document was composed much later and not by any Jewish conspiracy.
4. *Inconsistencies and Inaccuracies:* The text of *Protocols* is riddled with inconsistencies and inaccuracies. It refers to a global Jewish conspiracy for world domination, yet the Jewish community was highly fragmented and diverse during that time. The document also portrays Jews as having an unparalleled level of coordination, which historical reality contradicts.
5. *Debunking by Scholars:* Over the years, scholars, historians, and experts in various fields have exhaustively studied and analyzed the *Protocols*. Their research has consistently debunked the document's authenticity, highlighting the many sources of its plagiarized content and tracing its creation back to known antisemitic circles.

6. **Court Cases and Official Investigations:** In the early 20th century, several investigations and court cases were conducted to examine the authenticity of the *Protocols*. Notably, the Berne Trial in Switzerland (1933) concluded that the *Protocols* was a forgery created to spread antisemitic propaganda.
7. **Condemnation by Authorities:** Organizations such as the Anti-Defamation League (ADL) and historians from various backgrounds have consistently denounced the *Protocols* as a hoax. These condemnations are based on solid research, analysis, and historical evidence.

The bottom line is that numerous historical refutations of the *Protocols of the Elders of Zion* provide substantial evidence that the document is indeed a hoax and a forgery. It was fabricated with malicious intent to fuel antisemitic sentiment and conspiracy theories. The scholarly consensus is overwhelmingly against its authenticity.

IX
Jacobs and Weitzman identified key themes to discount each protocol from a Jewish perspective.

Steven Jacobs and Mark Weitzman responded to the *Protocols* by referring to Jewish teachings (rather than just relying on historical facts). Foundational to refuting the *Protocols* differently than all previous historically-based refutations, in *Dismantling the Big Lie: The Protocols of the Elders of Zion* (2003), they created a list of "Themes Addressed" to construct a catalog of the baseless charges against the Jews. The 52 unique key concepts and themes of antisemitism identified can be synthesized into eight topics and related concepts that motivated adults might relate to from their own personal experience. See the list of topics below.

1. **Education:** Authority and Power, Education, Family, Law, Lawyers.
2. **Finance:** Bonds, Gentiles Business, Gold = Money, Loans, Money lending, Stock Markets and Stock Exchanges, Taxes and Taxation, Usury.
3. **Human Rights:** Criminal Element, Freedom and Liberty, Gentiles as Slaves, Liberty, Ownership of Land, Slavery, Speech.
4. **Politics:** Internal Unrest and Discord Leading to War vs. Shalom/Peace, International Political Economic Conspiracy, Jewish Political Involvement, King of Israel, Kingship, Majority Rule, Political Power and Authority, Politics.

5. *Practice/Other:* Business as Cold and Heartless, Jewish Ethics, Liberalism, Masonry, Masonry/Freemasonry, Public Service.
6. *Propaganda:* Christianity and Non-Jewish Authorship, Document as Fiction, Gossip, Pornography, Press and Censorship, Press/Media as Tools, Publishing.
7. *Race/Ethnicity:* Gentiles, Jewish People, Arrogant and Corrupt, Jewish People's Relationship to Larger Society.
8. *Religion:* Chosenness/Election, Clergy, Evil, God, Judaism, Martyrdom, Obedience to Authority, Sages of Israel.

X
Yet, the Protocols continues to be widely translated, distributed, and cited to justify antisemitic acts.

Since it was first published in Russia in the early 20th century, the *Protocols of the Elders of Zion* has been widely discredited as a forgery. There are several reasons why the *Protocols* continues to be widely translated, distributed, and cited despite being a fabrication:

1. *Confirmation Bias:* People who already hold antisemitic beliefs may be drawn to the *Protocols* because they confirm their existing prejudices. The text provides a seemingly coherent narrative that reinforces these biases.
2. *Simplicity and Appeal:* Conspiracy theories often gain traction because they offer simple explanations for complex situations. The *Protocols* simplifies the perceived complexities of world events by attributing them to a single, malevolent group.
3. *Confirmation by Authority Figures:* When influential figures, such as politicians, religious leaders, or media personalities, lend credibility to the text by citing or endorsing it, it can further perpetuate its circulation.
4. *Dissemination through Propaganda:* Historically, governments and organizations with antisemitic agendas have actively promoted the *Protocols* as a tool to fuel hatred and justify discriminatory policies. State-sponsored dissemination can greatly amplify its reach.
5. *Fear and Uncertainty:* During times of social, economic, or political instability, people may be more susceptible to conspiracy theories as a way to explain or cope with uncertainties.

6. *Internet and Globalization:* The Internet has made it easier for misinformation to spread rapidly and globally. Online platforms provide a way for these ideas to reach a broader audience, and they can become part of echo chambers where like-minded individuals reinforce each other's beliefs.
7. *Selective Use:* Antisemitic individuals or groups may selectively use parts of the *Protocols* to advance their agendas while ignoring its fraudulent origins. This selective use can lend a veneer of legitimacy to their claims.
8. *Historical Legacy:* The text has a long history, and its influence has persisted over generations. This historical legacy can contribute to its continued presence in some circles.

Efforts to counter the spread of the *Protocols* and other forms of antisemitic content involve education, raising awareness about the document's fraudulent origins, promoting critical thinking skills, and fostering tolerance and understanding among diverse communities. Nonetheless, combating deeply entrenched conspiracy theories and prejudice remains a complex and ongoing challenge.

XI
The meaning of "chosen"—in Biblical times—does not imply any innate Jewish superiority but rather a responsibility to set an example.

In Biblical times, the concept of being "chosen" held a specific meaning within the context of Judaism that is often misunderstood as implying Jewish superiority. However, the deeper understanding of this term points more toward a unique responsibility rather than a claim of inherent superiority.

The idea of being "chosen" is rooted in the Hebrew Bible (the Old Testament), where God is depicted as having chosen the Israelites, the descendants of Abraham, to be His people and to fulfill a particular role in His divine plan. This concept is mainly found in the books of Genesis, Exodus, and Deuteronomy. The term "chosen" does not indicate that the Israelites were intrinsically better than or superior to other peoples; rather, it signifies a divine election for a specific purpose.

- **Responsibility and the Covenant:** The notion of being chosen is closely tied to the covenant that God established with the Israelites. This covenant entailed a mutual relationship in which God would protect and guide the Israelites, and in return they would follow His commandments and serve as a model of ethical and moral living. This responsibility to live according to God's laws was a central aspect of the chosen status. The Israelites were expected to exemplify a life centered on righteousness, justice, and compassion.
- **A Light to the Nations:** The idea of being chosen is often accompanied by the concept that the Israelites were meant to be a "light to the nations." This means that their chosen status was not about exclusivity or superiority but about projecting an example of ethical monotheism and moral conduct to the rest of the world. They were to inspire others through their actions, demonstrating how to live in accordance with God's teachings.
- **Prophetical Mission:** Prophets in the Hebrew Bible repeatedly emphasized that the chosen status came with a mission to spread God's message and advocate for justice. The prophets called on the Israelites to uphold their responsibilities and condemned them when they strayed from the path of righteousness. This further reinforces the idea that being chosen was not about inherent superiority but about fulfilling a particular role in God's plan.
- **Challenges and Trials:** The chosen status also subjected the Israelites to trials and challenges. They faced hardships and consequences when they failed to live up to their responsibilities. This indicates that the chosen status was not a guarantee of success or superiority but rather a call to live a demanding and purposeful life.

Within Judaism, the concept of being "chosen" does not imply any innate Jewish superiority. Instead, it signifies a unique responsibility to follow God's commandments, serve as a moral example, and fulfill a divine mission. The true essence of being chosen lies in the commitment to righteousness, justice, and ethical conduct rather than any assertion of superiority over other peoples.

XII
Holocaust inversion casts Israel, Israelis, and Jews as the "new Nazis" and Palestinians as the "new Jews."

"Holocaust inversion," which is also referred to as "Holocaust relativism," describes the use of a false and highly controversial analogy by some individuals, groups, or organizations to draw parallels between Israel's actions and Nazi Germany's atrocities during the Holocaust. This analogy casts Israelis and Jews as the aggressors or oppressors, while portraying Palestinians as victims analogous to the Jews during the Holocaust. Here's how this analogy is typically presented.

1. **Equating Israeli Policies with Nazi Atrocities:** Advocates of Holocaust inversion often draw parallels between Israeli government policies, particularly those related to the Israeli-Palestinian conflict, and Nazi actions during the Holocaust. This can involve comparing the construction of settlements, security measures, and military operations to Nazi actions, implying that Israelis are committing similar atrocities. This is not to deny that criticism of certain Israeli actions may be legitimate.
2. **Portraying Palestinians as Victims:** By using Holocaust inversion, proponents aim to present Palestinians as the modern-day victims, much like the Jews were during the Holocaust. This narrative suggests that Palestinians are subjected to oppression, discrimination, and violence similar to what Jews experienced under Nazi rule.
3. **Misuse of Holocaust History:** Critics argue that Holocaust inversion manipulates the memory of the Holocaust for political purposes. This analogy can be offensive and diminish the gravity of the Holocaust by drawing superficial comparisons between vastly different historical contexts.
4. **Impact on Holocaust Memory:** Holocaust inversion can undermine the uniqueness and horror of the Holocaust by using it as a rhetorical tool in contemporary political debates. Many argue that this is a form of Holocaust denial or distortion, as it falsely equates the suffering of victims with the actions of modern political actors.

It's important to note that Holocaust inversion is a contentious topic, and opinions on its validity and appropriateness vary widely. Many people, including Holocaust survivors, scholars, and human rights organizations, strongly oppose the use of Holocaust analogies in contemporary political debates, particularly when used to delegitimize the State of Israel or to downplay the historical significance of the Holocaust.

Critics of this analogy argue that it oversimplifies complex political and historical issues, undermines constructive dialogue, and perpetuates hatred and bias. Constructive discussions about the Israeli-Palestinian conflict should involve a nuanced understanding of historical context, current events, and a commitment to promoting peace, justice, and human rights for all parties involved.

XIII
To be "Jewish" means to engage in certain cultural practices and/or to follow a particular set of beliefs—to be "different" from non-Jews.

Being "Jewish" is a complex and multifaceted identity that encompasses various cultural, religious, historical, and social dimensions. It's important to note that Judaism is both a religious tradition and an ethnic or cultural identity, and different individuals and communities might emphasize different aspects of this identity.

- ***Religious Beliefs and Practices:*** Spanning over 3,500 years, Judaism is one of the world's oldest monotheistic religions, with a rich set of religious beliefs, practices, and traditions. Jewish religious beliefs are centered around the worship of one God and the adherence to commandments found in the Torah, the foundational text of Judaism, as well as to its changing interpretations over time. Observance of religious practices such as keeping kosher dietary laws, observing the Sabbath, and celebrating holidays like Passover and Hanukkah are central to Jewish religious identity.
- ***Cultural Identity:*** Beyond the religious aspects, being Jewish also involves a strong cultural component. This includes traditions, customs, literature, music, art, and cuisine that have developed over centuries. Jewish culture has been influenced by the various regions and societies where Jewish communities have lived, resulting in diverse cultural expressions around the world.
- ***Historical Identity:*** The Jewish people have a long and complex history marked by various challenges, including periods of persecution, diaspora, and dispersion. The historical experiences of Jews have contributed to a sense of shared identity and solidarity among Jewish communities.

- **Ethnic Identity:** For many individuals, being Jewish is also tied to an ethnic or ancestral identity. Some Jewish people may identify as part of a Jewish ethnic group, tracing their ancestry back to specific geographical regions. This ethnic identity can include aspects of shared history, language (such as Yiddish), and cultural practices.
- **Sense of Community:** Jewish identity often includes a sense of belonging to a global community of people who share a common history and set of values. This sense of community can be particularly strong given the historical challenges faced by Jewish communities.

It's important to recognize that there is no single definition of what it means to be Jewish, and different individuals and communities may interpret and express their Jewish identity in diverse ways. While some Jewish individuals may prioritize religious practices, others may emphasize cultural or historical connections. Additionally, there are secular and cultural Jews who identify with the cultural and historical aspects of Judaism without adhering to its religious practices. Thus, being "Jewish" isn't solely about engaging in certain practices or beliefs but encompasses a rich tapestry of religious, cultural, historical, and social elements that contribute to a diverse and multifaceted identity.

XIV
Antisemitism is increasingly difficult to identify: it has grown into a complicated web of hatred that encompasses multiple dimensions.

Antisemitism is a complex and multifaceted form of Jew hatred that has evolved over centuries. Its manifestations can be difficult to identify due to the various ways it is expressed and the subtlety with which it often operates. While the landscape of antisemitism is vast and nuanced, here are some key elements that contribute to its complicated web of hatred.

1. **Historical Roots:** Antisemitism has deep historical roots that date back centuries. It has been perpetuated through religious narratives, economic competition, and cultural differences. Understanding this historical context is crucial for recognizing its contemporary forms.
2. **Stereotypes:** Antisemitism is often fueled by harmful stereotypes that portray Jewish people as greedy, manipulative, power-hungry, or conspiratorial. These stereotypes are deeply ingrained in many societies and contribute to negative perceptions.

3. **Conspiracy Theories:** Antisemitism frequently involves conspiracy theories that attribute disproportionate influence or control to Jewish individuals or groups in various aspects of society, such as politics, finance, media, and entertainment. These conspiracy theories perpetuate a sense of mistrust and fear.
4. **Dual Loyalty Accusations:** Jewish individuals have historically been subjected to accusations of having dual loyalty, implying that they are more loyal to Israel or their Jewish identity than to their respective countries. This type of accusation can isolate and marginalize Jewish communities.
5. **Holocaust Denial and Distortion:** Denying or distorting the Holocaust is a form of antisemitism that seeks to undermine the suffering of millions of Jews during the Holocaust. Such actions downplay the historical reality of this unique atrocity.
6. **Anti-Zionism and Anti-Israel Sentiment:** While criticism of Israeli policies isn't inherently antisemitic, there are instances where anti-Zionism crosses over into antisemitism by questioning Israel's right to exist or using disproportionate condemnation that targets Israel while ignoring similar actions by other countries.
7. **Online and Digital Space:** Antisemitism has found new avenues of expression in the digital age. Online platforms can amplify hate speech, stereotypes, and conspiracy theories, reaching a global audience and making it difficult to track and address.
8. **Microaggressions:** Antisemitism can manifest through microaggressions, which are subtle and often unintentional expressions of prejudice that marginalize and demean Jewish individuals.
9. **Cultural and Religious Manifestations:** Antisemitism can infiltrate culture and religion, leading to discriminatory practices, vandalism of Jewish institutions, and even violence against Jewish individuals.
10. **Intersectionality:** Antisemitism can also intersect with other forms of prejudice, such as racism, sexism, and discrimination based on sexual orientation and gender identity. Addressing its complexity requires understanding these intersections.
11. **Language and Symbols:** Antisemitism can be encoded in coded language and symbols that mask its true intent. Millions of unsuspecting people easily spread this coded antisemitic messaging by sharing or liking it without being aware of the consequences of their actions. Such messaging requires careful analysis to decipher its meaning.

Given the complexity of antisemitism, it's essential to approach the topic with sensitivity and a willingness to learn. Combating antisemitism involves education, awareness, fostering inclusive societies, and promoting dialogue that challenges prejudiced beliefs and fosters understanding.

XV
Social media propagandists rapidly spread their message by adapting to local idioms, trending memes, and changing "codes," which escalates antisemitic thinking and behavior on a massive scale.

This point touches on a complex and concerning issue involving the manipulation of social media platforms for the spread of harmful content, including antisemitic messages. To date, social media propagandists use a variety of strategies to rapidly spread their message and adapt to local idioms, trending memes, and changing "codes" in order to escalate antisemitic thinking and behavior on a massive scale. Here are some of the tactics they might employ.

- *Algorithm Exploitation:* Social media platforms use algorithms that prioritize content based on engagement and relevance. Propagandists can exploit these algorithms by creating content that generates high levels of engagement, such as likes, shares, and comments. This can push their messages to a wider audience, including those who might not have been exposed to such content otherwise.
- *Co-opting Local Language and Idioms:* Adapting messages to local idioms, language, and cultural references makes them appear more relatable and authentic to users in specific regions. This helps content resonate better with local audiences, increasing the likelihood of sharing and engagement.
- *Trend Utilization:* Propagandists often leverage trending topics, hashtags, and memes to piggyback on existing conversations and amplify their own messages. By inserting their content into popular discussions, they can attract more attention and expand their reach.
- *Use of Memes and Visuals:* Memes and visual content are highly shareable and can convey complex ideas in a simple and often humorous way. Propagandists create visually appealing content that aligns with their narrative, making it more likely to be shared widely.

- *Manipulation of Codes and Dog Whistles:* Propagandists might employ coded language and symbols that are recognizable to their target audience but may not be immediately obvious to outsiders. This tactic allows them to communicate extremist ideas while maintaining a level of plausible deniability.
- *Infiltration of Online Communities:* Propagandists might also join and engage with online communities, forums, and social media groups to spread their content from within. This can make their messages appear more authentic and increase their influence over time.
- *Automation and Bots:* Automated accounts (bots) can rapidly share and amplify content, creating an illusion of widespread support. This can make the content seem more influential and popular than it actually is.
- *Cross-Platform Promotion:* Propagandists use multiple social media platforms to reach a wider audience. They repurpose content for different platforms and tailor their approach to suit the user behavior on each one.

Countering these tactics requires a multi-faceted approach involving technology, policy changes, education, and community efforts. Social media platforms need to strengthen their content moderation systems, algorithms, and reporting mechanisms. Governments, NGOs, and educational institutions can work together to raise awareness about the dangers of online propaganda and provide media literacy education to help users critically evaluate the content they encounter. It's essential to stay informed about these issues and promote a safe and respectful online environment for all users.

XVI
Increasing awareness of unbiased "lessons learned" is changing perspectives as we learn more from history repeating itself.

An increasing awareness of unbiased "lessons learned" from history, especially in the context of antisemitism, is having a profound impact on how societies and individuals perceive and respond to these issues. Here's how this awareness is changing perspectives.

- *Recognition of Patterns:* As historical events are studied more critically and objectively, patterns of behavior and systemic issues become more evident. This allows societies to recognize when history

is repeating itself, including instances of antisemitism. By identifying these patterns, societies can take early preventative measures to address and counteract such prejudices and discrimination.
2. **Educational Efforts:** Unbiased analysis of history's lessons learned enables educational institutions to provide more accurate and comprehensive curricula. This includes teaching students about the devastating consequences of antisemitism and other forms of discrimination, fostering empathy, and promoting critical thinking to prevent the propagation of hateful ideologies.
3. **Cultural Sensitivity:** Learning from history's mistakes encourages societies to develop greater cultural sensitivity and understanding. Recognizing the impacts of past discrimination leads to increased respect for diverse cultures and backgrounds, fostering a more inclusive and harmonious society.
4. **Political and Social Activism:** An unbiased examination of history's failures can fuel political and social activism aimed at eradicating antisemitism. This awareness can empower individuals and groups to speak out against hate speech, support policy changes, and actively promote tolerance and acceptance.
5. **International Cooperation:** Global awareness of history's lessons learned, especially concerning antisemitism, can foster international cooperation in combating discrimination. Nations and organizations can collaborate to develop strategies and initiatives that work collectively to counteract hate and prejudice on a global scale.
6. **Media and Popular Culture:** An increasing awareness of unbiased lessons learned can influence media representations and popular culture. Media outlets and creators may be more inclined to accurately depict historical events and challenges, thereby contributing to a more informed and empathetic public discourse.
7. **Policy and Legislation:** Informed by history's lessons, policymakers are more likely to develop and enforce legislation aimed at preventing discrimination, hate crimes, and systemic biases. This includes enacting laws that protect minority rights and hold perpetrators of hate accountable.
8. **Interfaith Dialogue:** The lessons of history can stimulate interfaith dialogue, encouraging open discussions among various religious and cultural groups. Such dialogue can help break down stereotypes, dispel misconceptions, and foster mutual respect and cooperation.

9. ***Remembrance and Commemoration:*** Increased awareness of history's mistakes prompts societies to remember and commemorate the victims of antisemitism and other forms of discrimination. Memorialization serves as a reminder of the consequences of unchecked hatred, encouraging future generations to prevent its resurgence.
10. ***Psychological Impact:*** An awareness of history's lessons can have a psychological impact on individuals, cultivating a sense of responsibility to prevent history from repeating itself. This can lead to personal commitments to combat prejudice and promote tolerance.

As such, an increasing awareness of unbiased "lessons learned" from history, particularly in the context of antisemitism, is changing perspectives by promoting critical thinking, empathy, tolerance, and proactive measures to prevent the repetition of past injustices. This awareness empowers societies to confront and combat discrimination, contributing to a more just and inclusive world.

XVII
The techniques and tools used to understand and combat antisemitism can be applied to other toxic "-isms," like ageism, sexism, racism, etc.

The techniques and tools used to understand and combat one form of discrimination, such as antisemitism, can certainly be applied to other forms of discrimination like ageism, sexism, racism, etc. While the specific context and nuances of each "-ism" may vary, the general principles and strategies for addressing them often overlap. Here are some ways in which the techniques and tools can be adapted.

- ***Education and Awareness:*** As in the case of antisemitism, raising awareness about the history, origins, and harmful effects of other "-isms" is crucial. Educational campaigns, workshops, seminars, and online resources can help people understand the roots and impacts of these biases.
- ***Research and Data Collection:*** Collecting data and conducting research to identify instances and patterns of ageism, sexism, etc., can provide empirical evidence of their existence and help in formulating effective strategies.
- ***Policy and Legislation:*** Enacting and enforcing laws against discrimination based on age, gender, race, and other factors can serve as a legal

framework to address these issues. This approach has been used effectively to combat various forms of discrimination, including anti-semitism.

- *Media Literacy:* Promoting media literacy can help individuals critically analyze and challenge stereotypes, biases, and negative portrayals in both traditional and new media, which can contribute to combating various forms of discrimination.
- *Intersectionality:* Recognizing that individuals can face multiple forms of discrimination simultaneously is important. Just as anti-semitism intersects with other prejudices, such as racism or homophobia, acknowledging intersectionality is vital in addressing ageism, sexism, and other "-isms."
- *Dialogue and Engagement:* Encouraging open and respectful discussions among diverse groups of people can foster understanding and empathy. This approach can be applied to all forms of discrimination to break down barriers and promote unity.
- *Community Building:* Creating safe spaces for affected communities and allies to come together, share experiences, and support one another is effective in combating discrimination in all its forms.
- *Empowerment and Representation:* Promoting representation of marginalized groups in various sectors, including media, politics, and leadership roles, can help challenge stereotypes and increase visibility.
- *Advocacy and Allyship:* Encouraging individuals to become allies and advocate for change is a powerful tool. Just as combating antisemitism requires allies from different backgrounds, addressing other "-isms" benefits from diverse support.
- *Institutional Change:* Addressing systemic discrimination often requires changes within institutions and organizations. Diversity and inclusion initiatives can be adapted to tackle different forms of prejudice.
- *Long-Term Efforts:* Just as antisemitism is an ongoing concern, combating other forms of discrimination requires sustained efforts over time. Regular evaluation and adaptation of strategies is essential.

By adapting these techniques and tools, society can work toward combating various forms of discrimination, fostering inclusivity, and creating a more equitable and just environment for all individuals.

XVIII
Even though the term is used generically to describe genocides and other catastrophes, the Holocaust was a singular historical event.

The Holocaust, often referred to as the Shoah, was a singular and unprecedented historical event due to several significant factors.

1. *Scale and Systematic Nature:* The Holocaust was the uniquely industrialized and state-sponsored genocide orchestrated by Nazi Germany during World War II. It involved the systematic mass murder of over six million Jews, as well as millions of other individuals including Roma, disabled persons, political dissidents, homosexuals, and others considered undesirable by the Nazi regime. The scale and organized nature of the killings set the Holocaust apart from all other instances of mass violence.
2. *Ideological Motivation:* The Holocaust was driven by a deeply ingrained ideological belief in the racial superiority of the Aryan race (with Germans as the master race) and the elimination of a perceived racial and ethnic enemy: the Jews. The Nazi regime implemented a comprehensive plan to annihilate the entire Jewish population based on their ethnicity and beliefs, which makes the Holocaust unique in terms of its ideological underpinnings.
3. *Bureaucratic Efficiency:* The Nazi regime established a highly efficient bureaucratic machinery to carry out the Holocaust. This included the construction of concentration camps, extermination camps, and ghettos, as well as the development of methods for mass murder such as gas chambers. A combination of ideological fervor, meticulous organization, and detailed record-keeping, as well as a high level of local complicity, resulted in a level of brutality and death on an unprecedented scale.
4. *Global Impact:* The Holocaust had a profound impact on global consciousness and the international human rights discourse. It led to the establishment of new international laws and norms to prevent such atrocities from occurring again, including the United Nations' adoption of the Genocide Convention in 1948. The Holocaust also played a role in shaping discussions on human rights, tolerance, and the importance of preventing discrimination and bigotry, as well as on the importance of individual decision-making in preventing discrimination and bigotry from taking root in societies.

5. ***Cultural and Educational Significance:*** The Holocaust has become a focal point for education, remembrance, and research. Efforts to document survivor testimonies, historical records, and artifacts have contributed to a deeper understanding of the events that transpired, including the degree of complicity of the general public. Educational programs and museums worldwide seek to ensure that the memory of the Holocaust remains alive and serves as a stark reminder of the consequences of unchecked hatred and prejudice.
6. ***Symbol of Inhumanity:*** The Holocaust stands as the universal symbol of the darkest depths of human cruelty and intolerance. It highlights the potential for individuals and societies to commit horrific acts when driven by a toxic combination of ideology, power, and indifference.
7. ***Ethical and Moral Lessons:*** The Holocaust serves as a stark reminder of the ethical and moral responsibilities that individuals and societies have toward each other. It prompts reflection on the importance of combating discrimination, promoting tolerance, and safeguarding human dignity.

It is of utmost importance to recognize that the Holocaust's *singularity* lies in its state sponsorship, unprecedented scale, systematic nature, ideological motivation, bureaucratic efficiency, and global impact. The Holocaust was a catastrophic rupture in human civilization. While the term "holocaust" (with a small "h") has been used generically to describe other instances of mass violence, the historical specificity and magnitude of the Holocaust (with a capital "H") set it apart as a unique and uniquely significant event in human history.

At the same time, the *universality* of the Holocaust highlights the global relevance of its lessons, emphasizing the need for collective responsibility, education, and vigilance in safeguarding human rights and preventing genocide and mass atrocities. It underscores the importance of remembering the past to build a more just and tolerant future.

XIX

People will always have their differences, but they share a common set of emotions and a capacity for self-awareness, abstract thinking, computational abilities, and knowing right from wrong.

While people may have various cultural, social, and individual differences, there are certain fundamental aspects that are shared across human beings. These common traits and capacities include:

- *Emotions:* Humans universally experience a range of emotions such as happiness, sadness, anger, fear, and love. While the specific triggers and expressions of these emotions can vary, the underlying experiences are similar.
- *Self-Awareness:* Humans possess the ability to be aware of themselves as individuals with thoughts, feelings, and intentions. This self-awareness allows them to reflect on their own actions and thoughts.
- *Abstract Thinking:* People can engage in abstract thinking, which involves conceptualizing and manipulating ideas that are not directly tied to sensory experiences. This capacity enables them to create complex systems of thought, solve problems, and develop new concepts.
- *Computational Abilities:* While the extent of computational abilities can vary among individuals, humans generally possess the cognitive capacity to process information, make decisions, and solve problems using logical reasoning and various other mental processes.
- *Moral and Ethical Understanding:* Humans have a general understanding of right and wrong, although the specifics of moral values can differ across cultures and individuals. This understanding forms the basis for developing empathy, ethical decision-making, and social interactions.

These shared traits form the foundation for communication, cooperaion, and the development of societies. They are essential components of vhat makes us human, fostering connections and allowing us to under-;tand and relate to each other despite our differences.

XX
While antisemitism is an overwhelming global issue, what you do in your own sphere of influence makes a difference: be an upstander.

Addressing contemporary antisemitism requires a collective effort, and individuals can play a significant role in making a positive difference in their own spheres of influence. Here are some steps you can take.

1. *Education and Awareness:* Educate yourself about the history of antisemitism, its different forms, and its impact on individuals and communities. Share accurate information and resources with friends, family, and colleagues to raise awareness about the issue.
2. *Challenge Stereotypes:* Be vigilant about the language you use and the stereotypes you may inadvertently perpetuate. Avoid making jokes or comments that reinforce negative stereotypes about Jewish people. Challenge others when you hear or see antisemitic comments or behavior, in a respectful and informative manner.
3. *Foster Inclusion:* Create an inclusive environment where diversity is celebrated and respected. Encourage open dialogue that allows people to share their experiences and perspectives without fear of discrimination. Promote initiatives that highlight the contributions of Jewish individuals and communities to various fields.
4. *Support Jewish Organizations:* Contribute to and support organizations that are actively working to combat antisemitism promote tolerance, and educate the public. Attend events, lectures and workshops organized by Jewish cultural, religious, and educational institutions to gain a deeper understanding.
5. *Promote Interfaith Dialogue:* Engage in interfaith dialogue to foster understanding and collaboration among different religious and cultural communities. Attend or organize events that bring people of different faiths together to share experiences and build relationships.
6. *Speak Out:* Use your platform, whether it's social media, local community groups, or workplace discussions, to speak out against antisemitism and other forms of hate speech. Advocate for policies and legislation that promote tolerance and protect minority rights.
7. *Report Hate Incidents:* If you witness or experience antisemitic behavior, report it to the appropriate authorities or organizations that track hate incidents. Encourage others to report hate incidents as well.

as this helps gather data and raise awareness about the extent of the problem.
8. **Support Holocaust Education:** Support educational programs and institutions that teach about the Holocaust and its lessons on the dangers of unchecked prejudice and hatred.
9. **Lead by Example:** Model respectful behavior and empathy for others in your interactions. Show others how to treat all individuals with dignity and respect, regardless of their background.
10. **Engage in Personal Reflection:** Reflect on your own biases and prejudices. Work on recognizing and challenging them to create a more inclusive mindset.

Remember that creating change takes time, persistence, and a collective effort. By taking these steps, you can contribute to a more tolerant and inclusive society, helping to combat antisemitism and other forms of discrimination.

2. IDENTIFYING PROPAGANDA

An understanding of propaganda techniques is a powerful tool for upstanders in the fight against conspiracy theories and antisemitism. By using this knowledge to identify, debunk, and counteract propaganda, individuals and communities can contribute to a more informed and tolerant society. Here's how this understanding can be applied.

- **Identification of Manipulation:** Knowledge of propaganda techniques helps individuals recognize when they are being manipulated or when others are being targeted with misinformation. This recognition is essential in the fight against conspiracy theories, which often rely on distorted facts and emotionally charged narratives.
- **Critical Thinking:** Upstanders armed with an understanding of propaganda techniques are better equipped to critically evaluate information and claims. They can ask questions such as, "Is this information based on credible sources?" or "Is this argument using emotional appeal or logical reasoning?" Critical thinking can expose the weaknesses in conspiracy theories and help individuals see through their fallacies.

- **Media Literacy:** Propaganda often relies on misusing media platforms. Knowing how propaganda spreads through social media, traditional media, or word-of-mouth can help upstanders identify and report suspicious content. Promoting media literacy education can also be an effective way to inoculate people against conspiracy theories.
- **Debunking Myths:** Armed with knowledge about propaganda techniques, upstanders can effectively debunk conspiracy theories by pointing out the specific tactics being used. They can explain how emotional manipulation, cherry-picked evidence, or logical fallacies are employed to create and perpetuate false narratives.
- **Offering Alternative Narratives:** Upstanders can counter conspiracy theories by providing well-researched, fact-based alternative narratives. These narratives should be presented clearly and effectively to appeal to the same emotional and psychological factors that conspiracy theories exploit.
- **Promoting Critical Dialogue:** Encourage open and respectful dialogue between individuals who hold conspiracy beliefs and those who seek to challenge them. When upstanders approach these conversations with empathy and a firm grasp of propaganda techniques, they can be more effective in helping people reconsider their beliefs.
- **Supporting Education Initiatives:** Propaganda and conspiracy theories often thrive in environments where critical thinking skills are lacking. Supporting educational programs that teach media literacy, critical thinking, and fact-checking can be instrumental in combating the spread of antisemitic conspiracy theories.
- **Collaboration:** Upstanders should collaborate with organizations and experts who specialize in countering propaganda and conspiracy theories. These organizations often have resources, research, and strategies that can be highly effective in addressing these issues.
- **Vigilance:** Recognizing that propaganda and conspiracy theories can evolve over time, upstanders should remain vigilant and adapt their strategies as needed. Continuously educate yourself about new propaganda tactics and conspiracy theories that may emerge.
- **Community Building:** Creating strong, inclusive communities can help counter antisemitism and the appeal of conspiracy theories. When people feel connected and supported within their communities, they are less susceptible to extremist ideologies and more open to alternative perspectives.

Propaganda Techniques

PBS's *Reporting America at War* educator materials summarize core content adapted from the *Propaganda Critic* website, as follows:

PROPAGANDA – the use of a variety of communication techniques that create an emotional appeal to accept a particular belief or opinion, to adopt a certain behavior or to perform a particular action. There is some disagreement about whether all persuasive communication is propagandistic or whether the propaganda label can only be applied to dishonest messages.

NAME CALLING – links a person, or idea, to a negative symbol. Examples: commie, fascist, yuppie

GLITTERING GENERALITIES – use of virtue words; the opposite of name calling, i.e., links a person, or idea, to a positive symbol. Examples: democracy, patriotism, family

The next two are ways of making false connections:

TRANSFER – a device by which the propagandist links the authority or prestige of something well-respected and revered, such as church or nation, to something he would have us accept. Example: a political activist closes her speech with a prayer

TESTIMONIAL – a public figure or a celebrity promotes or endorses a product, a policy, or a political candidate. Examples: an athlete appears on the Wheaties box; an actor speaks at a political rally

The following three constitute special appeals:

PLAIN FOLKS – attempt to convince the audience that a prominent person and his ideas are "of the people." Examples: a prominent politician eats at McDonald's; an actress is photographed shopping for groceries

BANDWAGON – makes the appeal that "everyone else is doing it, and so should you." Examples: an ad states that "everyone is rushing down to their Ford dealer"

FEAR – plays on deep-seated fears; warns the audience that disaster will result if they do not follow a particular course of action. Example: an insurance company pamphlet includes pictures of houses destroyed [by] floods, followed up by details about home-owners' insurance.

The next two are types of logical fallacies:

BAD LOGIC – an illogical message is not necessarily propagandistic; it can be just a logical mistake; it is propaganda if logic is manipulated deliberately to promote a cause. Example: Senator X wants to regulate the power industry.

All Communist governments regulate their power industries. Senator X is a Communist.

UNWARRANTED EXTRAPOLATION – making huge predictions about the future on the basis of a few small facts. Example: If the U.S. approves NAFTA, thousands of jobs and factories will move to Mexico.

Artificial Intelligence (AI) Impacts

Artificial intelligence (AI) can have a significant impact on disguising and disseminating antisemitic ideas, just as it can with any other form of hate speech or harmful content. In today's digital world, one must also consider how language models affect the future of influence operations. In "Generative Language Models and Automated Influence Operations: Emerging Threats and Potential Mitigations," Goldstein et al. (2023) investigated how language models can affect which actors wage influence operations and what content they produce.

Actors: Language models drive down the cost of generating propaganda—the deliberate attempt to shape perceptions and direct behavior to further an actor's interest—so more actors may find it attractive to wage these campaigns. Likewise, propagandists-for-hire that automate production of text may gain new competitive advantages.

Behavior: Recent AI models can generate synthetic text that is highly scalable, and often highly persuasive. Influence operations with language models will become easier to scale, and more expensive tactics (e.g., generating personalized content) may become cheaper. Moreover, language models could enable new tactics to emerge—like real-time content generation in one-on-one chatbots.

Content: Language models may create more impactful messaging compared to propagandists who lack linguistic or cultural knowledge of their target. They may also make influence operations less discoverable, since they create new content with each generation.

When considering these predicted changes, it is also important to remember that AI development is progressing rapidly. [Critical unknowns will] impact the future of influence operations, including how models will improve, whether new capabilities will emerge as a product of scale, whether actors invest in AI for influence operations, and whether norms emerge that constrain different actors from automating their influence campaigns.

To combat the potentially negative impacts of AI on the dissemination of antisemitic ideas, several strategies and countermeasures can be employed, including:

- **Content Moderation:** Platforms should invest in advanced AI and machine learning tools to detect and remove hate speech and antisemitic content proactively.
- **Transparency and Accountability:** Tech companies should be transparent about their content moderation policies and practices. Additionally, there should be mechanisms for users to report problematic content.
- **Ethical AI Development:** Developers should adhere to ethical guidelines when designing AI systems and consider the potential negative societal impacts of their creations.
- **Media Literacy:** Promoting media literacy and critical thinking skills can help individuals better discern between credible and harmful content.
- **Regulation:** Governments may need to enact regulations that hold tech companies accountable for the content on their platforms and incentivize them to take stronger actions against hate speech.
- **AI for Good:** Encourage the development of AI tools and technologies that can help counter hate speech and promote tolerance, such as AI-powered content analysis tools.

3. STRATEGIES FOR "THINKING THROUGH" ISSUES

Offering a concrete way to suspend the emotional judgments that often cloud matters of ideology, Edward de Bono's focus on the development of thinking skills can support a shift to inquiry-based learning and thinking for problem-solving. These kinds of thinking tools can motivate people to suspend their emotional judgment, think much more broadly, and reach conclusions that are relevant to their own time and place. The following sections describe three of de Bono's basic operationalized thinking skills that are useful in fighting antisemitism. To learn more about these and other thinking skills, visit de Bono Thinking Systems at https://www.deBono.com.

PMI: The Treatment of Ideas

PMI embodies an open-minded approach in a practical tool. It's a fundamental first thinking lesson. Rather than simply judging an idea positively or negatively, this cognitive process prompts individuals to actively seek out its merits (P = Plus), drawbacks (M = Minus), and intriguing aspects (I = Interesting). The "Interesting" category encompasses aspects neither inherently good nor bad, yet worth acknowledging.

PMI serves as a method for evaluating ideas, suggestions, and proposals. Typically, our immediate response to an idea leans towards liking or disliking it, thereby overlooking opposing viewpoints. By employing PMI deliberately, thinkers can move beyond their initial reactions, transitioning from a defensive stance to a more explorative mindset.

Importantly, PMI isn't meant to hinder decision-making or commitment but to ensure that decisions are made only after considering both sides of the issue thoroughly. In essence, PMI broadens perspectives on a situation; without it, emotional reactions tend to narrow one's viewpoint.

CAF: Consider All Factors

Consider All Factors (CAF) represents the distilled essence of systematically considering all elements within a given scenario. This cognitive process is intricately linked to action, decision-making, planning, judgment, and reaching conclusions.

While individuals often believe they have thoroughly considered all elements, their examination typically only extends to the most apparent factors. Transforming CAF into a deliberate practice shifts the focus from the importance of individual factors to actively seeking out all elements. Given the challenge of comprehensively considering all factors, it's helpful to structure thinking around factors impacting oneself, others, or society at large.

While PMI reacts to specific ideas, CAF delves into situational exploration before idea formulation. Although there is occasional overlap between the two, as some factors naturally have positive or negative aspects, CAF's primary aim is completeness, considering all factors impartially rather than evaluating them as favorable or unfavorable.

OPV: Other People's Views

Other People's Views (OPV) represents the distilled essence of actively considering the viewpoints of others, allowing for a conscious and intentional utilization of this process. Unlike PMI and CAF, this expansion of understanding—broadening of perception—involves the thinking of multiple individuals.

Being able to comprehend and appreciate another person's perspective is a crucial aspect of the thinking process. Therefore, a deliberate effort might be necessary to adopt another viewpoint. Once thinkers can shift away from their own viewpoints, they can begin to take others into account, potentially uncovering valuable new insights into a situation.

OPV acts as a remedy to self-centeredness. Instead of merely acknowledging in a vague sense that others' perspectives matter, there's an intentional effort to understand another person's viewpoint.

The focus should be on illustrating how another person's perspective in the same situation may diverge significantly. It's the potential disparity in viewpoints that holds significance. Assuming that any sensible person would share the same viewpoint in a given situation undermines the necessity of making an effort to understand other perspectives.

4. PRACTICAL RESOURCES FOR INITIATING CHANGE

When dealing with sensitive and complex issues like antisemitism or other forms of discrimination, it's essential to approach the topic with care and diligence. In learning about complex and sensitive issues like antisemitism and other toxic "-isms," relying on vetted primary sources (as suggested in the following sections) helps ensure that you have the most accurate, nuanced, and trustworthy information to inform your understanding and decision-making. This is critical for several reasons:

- **Accuracy and Credibility:** Primary sources are original materials that provide firsthand accounts, data, or evidence about a topic. They are typically more accurate and credible than secondary or tertiary sources because they are closest to the original event or idea. When dealing with sensitive topics like discrimination or prejudice, accuracy is paramount to avoid spreading misinformation or reinforcing harmful stereotypes.

- *Avoiding Bias and Misinterpretation:* Secondary sources, such as news articles or opinion pieces, can be influenced by the biases and perspectives of authors or media outlets. Relying solely on these sources may lead to a skewed understanding of the issue. Primary sources, on the other hand, allow individuals to form their own interpretations and avoid relying on someone else's perspective.
- *Context and Nuance:* Many complex issues, including antisemitism and other "-isms," require a deep understanding of the historical, cultural, and societal context. Primary sources often provide this context, helping individuals grasp the nuances of the issue. Without context, it's easy to misinterpret or oversimplify complex matters.
- *Depth of Information:* Primary sources tend to offer a more in-depth exploration of a topic. They often include a variety of perspectives and details that secondary sources may omit or simplify. This depth is crucial for gaining a comprehensive understanding of the issue and making informed decisions.
- *Authenticity and Trustworthiness:* Primary sources are less susceptible to manipulation, fabrication, or misrepresentation than secondary sources. Their authenticity and trustworthiness are particularly important when dealing with issues that may be sensitive or controversial.
- *Critical Thinking and Analysis:* Engaging with primary sources requires critical thinking skills. It encourages individuals to question, evaluate, and analyze the information presented. This process fosters intellectual growth and a deeper understanding of the issue at hand.
- *Academic and Professional Standards:* In academic and professional settings, using primary sources is often expected and even required. It demonstrates a commitment to rigorous research and intellectual integrity.
- *Avoiding Propaganda and Manipulation:* Primary sources are less likely to be influenced by propaganda or bias, making them a more reliable source of information, especially in cases where misinformation campaigns may be at play.

Recommended Websites

The following websites offer informative perspectives on contemporary antisemitism.

Anti-Defamation League, https://www.adl.org
ADL is the world's leading anti-hate organization. Founded in 1913, its timeless mission is "to stop the defamation of the Jewish people and to secure justice and fair treatment to all." Today, ADL continues to fight all forms of antisemitism and bias, using innovation and partnerships to drive impact. A global leader in combating antisemitism, countering extremism, and battling bigotry wherever and whenever it happens, ADL works to protect democracy and ensure a just and inclusive society for all.

Facing History & Ourselves, https://www.facinghistory.org
Facing History & Ourselves uses lessons of history to challenge teachers and their students to stand up to bigotry and hate. From one classroom in Brookline, Massachusetts in 1976, Facing History & Ourselves has become a global organization with a network of hundreds of thousands of middle and secondary school educators reaching millions of students worldwide. They help educators prepare students to participate in civic life—using intellect, empathy, ethics, and choice to stand up to bigotry and hate in their own lives, communities, and schools.

Institute for the Study of Global Antisemitism and Policy, https://isgap.org
The Institute for the Study of Global Antisemitism and Policy (ISGAP) is committed to fighting antisemitism on the battlefield of ideas. ISGAP is dedicated to scholarly research into the origins, processes, and manifestations of global antisemitism and other forms of prejudice, including various forms of racism, as they relate to policy in an age of globalization. On the basis of this examination of antisemitism and policy, ISGAP disseminates analytical and scholarly materials to help combat hatred and promote understanding.

International Holocaust Remembrance Alliance, https://www.holocaustremembrance.com
The International Holocaust Remembrance Alliance (IHRA) unites governments and experts to strengthen, advance, and promote Holocaust education, research, and remembrance and to uphold the commitments to the 2000 Stockholm Declaration. The IHRA's network of trusted experts share their knowledge on early warning signs of present-day genocide and education on the Holocaust. This

knowledge supports policymakers and educational multipliers in their efforts to develop effective curricula, and it informs government officials and NGOs active in global initiatives for genocide prevention.

Southern Poverty Law Center, https://www.splcenter.org

The US-based Southern Poverty Law Center (SPLC) is a catalyst for racial justice in the South and beyond, working in partnership with communities to dismantle white supremacy, strengthen intersectional movements, and advance the human rights of all people. Its lawsuits have toppled institutional racism and stamped out remnants of Jim Crow segregation; destroyed some of the nation's most violent white supremacist groups; and protected the civil rights of children, women, the disabled, immigrants and migrant workers, the LGBTQ community, prisoners, and many others who faced discrimination, abuse or exploitation.

United States Holocaust Memorial Museum, https://www.ushmm.org

A living memorial to the Holocaust, the United States Holocaust Memorial Museum (USHMM) inspires citizens and leaders worldwide to confront hatred, prevent genocide, and promote human dignity. Federal support guarantees the Museum's permanent place on the National Mall, and its far-reaching educational programs and global impact are made possible by generous donors.

Recommended Books

The following books offer informative perspectives on antisemitism.

Steven Beller, ***Antisemitism: A Very Short Introduction***, Oxford University Press, 2007.

This book focuses on antisemitism as a political movement and ideology: how it arose in Central Europe in the late 19th century and how its ideological claims became integrated into European and Western political, but also social, intellectual, and cultural life, which ultimately led to the Holocaust.

Herman Bernstein, ***The History of a Lie***, Ogilvie, 1921.

Bernstein's book was one of the very first refutations of the *Protocol of the Elders of Zion* to be widely read. He traced the origins of the *Protocols* to a French political pamphlet published in 1864. He also showed that the *Protocols* was plagiarized from other fictional sources and that they contained many factual errors. Around the same time, Bernstein instituted a libel suit (which he won) against Henry Ford and *The Dearborn Independent* for publishing the *Protocols*. Bernstein (1876–1935) was an author, translator, journalist, communal activist, and diplomat, who among many important positions served as a correspondent for the *New York Herald* in Russia in 1917–1920 and at the Paris Peace Conference in 1919. In the 1920s, he also served as secretary of the American Jewish Committee.

Dara Horn, **People Love Dead Jews: Reports from a Haunted Present**, W.W. Norton & Company, 2021.

Horn's work presents a powerful, uncomfortable insight into the way we have been conditioned to remember Jewish history. She highlights Holocaust memory efforts as focusing wrongly on embracing universal lessons instead of keeping the focus on the actual persecution of Jews. She sees all these ways of "remembering" as distractions from the main issue—which is "the very concrete, specific death of Jews." Horn points out the danger of thinking in certain ways, which sets limits on what can or cannot be said. Focusing on the upswell of antisemitism in the United States, Horn discusses the use of the Holocaust as the "high bar" set for antisemitism, making it much easier to see every antisemitic "happening" today as being "less than the Holocaust" and therefore much easier to dismiss. The Holocaust, in her words, "only happened because entire societies abdicated responsibility for their own problems, and instead blamed them on the people who represented—have always represented, since they first introduced the idea of commandedness to the world—the thing they were so afraid of: responsibility" (p. 191).

Steven Jacobs and Mark Weitzman, **Dismantling the Big Lie: The Protocols of the Elders of Zion,** Simon Wiesenthal Center in association with KTAV Publishing House Inc., 2003.

This refutation of the *Protocols* uniquely deploys Jewish scripture, from the Talmud, the Zohar, and the Mishnah, to refute the *Protocols*. In disproving the *Protocols'* claim to expose a hidden conspiracy, Jacobs and Weitzman refute each *Protocol* item by item, word for word, and line by line. They do this by using what authentic Jewish texts, teachings, and traditions say about all the questions raised about the Jews in each of the *Protocols*.

Garth Jowett and Victoria O'Donnell, ***Propaganda & Persuasion***, 7th ed., SAGE Publications, 2018.
With the ever-growing use of global propaganda and the Internet, this work presents a comprehensive history of propaganda and offers insightful definitions and methods to analyze it. Jowett and O'Donnell provide a clear understanding of persuasion and propaganda, including communication history, rhetorical background, cultural studies, and collective memory.

Matthias Küntzel, ***Nazis, Islamic Antisemitism and the Middle East: The 1948 Arab War against Israel and the Aftershocks of World War II***, Routledge, 2023.
Küntzel explores the still under-analyzed impact of Nazi antisemitism on the development of Islamic antisemitism and the Arab world's 1948 war against Israel. He makes the case for clear connections between the Nazi war of extermination against the Jews that ended in May 1945 and the war of the Arab armies against Israel that started in May 1948. This finding calls into question the belief that the Arab movement against Zionism and Israel had nothing to do with genocidal antisemitism and that the Jews—not just Israel—were mainly responsible for the 1948 war and antisemitism in the entire region.

Richard Landes, ***Can "The Whole World" Be Wrong?" Lethal Journalism, Antisemitism, and Global Jihad***, Academic Studies Press, 2022.
Landes is a medievalist and historian who specializes in medieval millennial thinking. Landes takes readers through the first years of the 21st millennium (2000–2003). He identifies in detail the ideas and people responsible for the upsurge of hostility and aggression towards Jewish people in recent years. He helps us to understand that this is occurring within the larger framework of extremist anti-democratic ideologies, movements, and mindsets. Landes documents how Western misinterpretations and radical inability to understand the medieval mentality that drive global jihad have played a fundamental role in exacerbating the moral and empirical disorientation of our information elites, including journalists, academics, and pundits. Landes demonstrates how this pattern of amplifying both Palestinian and jihadi war propaganda effectively undermines the credibility and integrity of journalistic coverage. He explains that this has led to widespread public skepticism towards information sources, deep socio-political divisions within democratic societies, the politicization of scientific discourse, and the inability of Western elites to effectively defend their own civilization.

INDEX

ADL, 18, 43
artificial intelligence, 38
authority, 18–19, 37

bias, 2, 14, 23, 28–30, 35, 43
biased, 7
confirmation bias, 19

Chosen, 20–21
Christianity, 19
combatting antisemitism, 3, 11, 26, 30, 43
conspiracy, 2, 4, 7, 9–11, 13–16, 18–19, 20, 25, 35–36, 45
conspiracy theory, 13
court, 16, 18
critical thinking, 12, 20, 28–29, 35–36, 39
cultural, 7, 10, 16, 23–25, 26, 28, 32–34, 38, 44, 46

dialogue, 3, 23, 26, 28, 30, 34, 36
discrimination, 2–4, 7, 9–13, 15–16, 22, 25, 28–32, 34–35, 44
Dreyfus, 7

education, 3, 18, 20, 26–29, 32, 34–36, 43–44

fear, 19, 25, 33–34, 37

hate, 3–4, 12–13, 16, 25, 28, 34, 39, 43
Henry Ford, 14, 45

historical, 2, 5, 10, 12, 17–20, 22–25, 27–28, 31–32
hoax, 4, 10, 12–13, 17–18
Holocaust, 2, 4, 7, 9, 22–25, 31–32, 35, 43–45
  memory, 22, 45
  singularity, 32
  universality, 32

identity, 3, 7, 23–25
IHRA, 8, 43
inclusivity, 3, 30
Intersectionality, 3, 7, 25, 30
Israel, 2, 7–9, 18–19, 22–23, 25, 46
Israeli/Israelite, 3, 7, 9, 20–22

media literacy, 12, 27, 30, 36, 39
misinformation, 10, 15, 20, 35
money, 18
  moneylenders, 5

persecution, 2, 4, 16, 23, 45
plagiarism, 17
  plagiarized, 15, 17, 44
pogroms, 2, 7
prejudice, 2–4, 7, 10–13, 19–20, 25–26, 28–30, 35, 43
propaganda, 3–4, 11–15, 18–19, 27, 35–38, 46
public opinion, 12, 13, 15

racism, 3, 10, 25, 29–30, 43–44
religious, 7–8, 10, 16, 19, 23–25, 28, 34

Russia, 4, 12, 14–15, 17, 22, 45

scapegoat, 4, 13, 15, 17
  scapegoating, 12
social, 7, 11, 15–16, 19, 23–24, 28, 33, 44
  Socalist, 9
  social media, 3, 26–27, 34, 36
stereotypes, 2–4, 7–8, 10, 12–13, 24–25, 28, 30, 34

tolerance, 2–4, 7, 13, 20, 28–29, 31–32, 34, 39
  intolerance, 10–11, 32

United Nations, 7, 31
upstander, 1, 34–36

victims, 3, 22, 29
vigilance, 4, 32, 36

Wiesel, 10–11

xenophobia, 3

Zionism, 46
  anti-Zionism, 25

POINTS TO REMEMBER

THE BIG LIE
1. Antisemitism is the only form of racism that's grounded in a conspiracy theory.
2. Antisemitism started with the Jews, but it won't end with the Jews...
3. While propaganda isn't always negative, the *Protocols of the Elders of Zion* is an example of the worst kind of propaganda.
4. The core of contemporary antisemitism, the *Protocols* is a fabricated story that blames the Jewish people for all of the world's problems.
5. As Henry Ford said, "they [the *Protocols*] fit in with what is going on," but if you *think* about it they're just a "convenient" excuse for other factors.

THE PROTOCOLS
6. The *Protocols* was crafted to protect the Russian Tsar's political position.
7. The simple pamphlet details a fictitious Jewish plot to take over the world.
8. Numerous historical refutations prove that the 24 protocols are a hoax.
9. Jacobs and Weitzman identified key themes to discount each protocol from a Jewish perspective.
10. Yet, the *Protocols* continues to be widely translated, distributed, and cited to justify antisemitic acts.

ANTISEMITISM
11. The meaning of "chosen"—in Biblical times—does not imply any innate Jewish superiority but rather a responsibility to set an example.
12. Holocaust inversion casts Israel, Israelis, and Jews as the "new Nazis" and Palestinians as the "new Jews."
13. To be "Jewish" means to engage in certain cultural practices and/or to follow a particular set of beliefs—to be "different" from non-Jews.
14. Antisemitism is increasingly difficult to identify: it has grown into a complicated web of hatred that encompasses multiple dimensions.
15. Social media propagandists rapidly spread their message by adapting to local idioms, trending memes, and changing "codes," which escalates antisemitic thinking and behavior on a massive scale.

BREAKING PROTOCOL
16. Increasing awareness of unbiased "lessons learned" is changing perspectives as we learn more from history repeating itself.
17. The techniques and tools used to understand and combat antisemitism can be applied to other toxic "-isms," like ageism, sexism, racism, etc.
18. Even though the term is used generically to describe genocides and other catastrophes, the Holocaust was a singular historical event.
19. People will always have their differences, but they share a common set of emotions and a capacity for self-awareness, abstract thinking, computational abilities, and knowing right from wrong.
20. While antisemitism is an overwhelming global issue, what you do in your own sphere of influence makes a difference: be an upstander.

Made in the USA
Middletown, DE
04 July 2024

56637698R00031